THE Golden Touch

Nicolas Brasch
Amanda Dawson

Australia • Brazil • Japan • Korea • Mexico • Singapore • Spain • United Kingdom • United States

The Golden Touch

Fast Forward
Orange Level 15

Text: Nicolas Brasch
Illustrations: Amanda Dawson
Editor: Cameron Macintosh
Design: James Lowe
Series design: James Lowe
Production controller: Emma Hayes
Audio recordings: Juliet Hill, Picture Start
Spoken by: Matthew King and Abbe Holmes
Reprint: Jennifer Foo

ISBN 978 0 17 012599 4
ISBN 978 0 17 012597 0 (set)

Cengage Learning Australia
Level 7, 80 Dorcas Street
South Melbourne, Victoria Australia 3205
Phone: 1300 790 853

Cengage Learning New Zealand
Unit 4B Rosedale Office Park
331 Rosedale Road, Albany, North Shore NZ 0632
Phone: 0800 449 725

For learning solutions, visit **cengage.com.au**

Printed in Australia by Ligare Pty Ltd
7 8 9 10 11 12 13 21 20 19 18 17

Evaluated in independent research by staff from the Department of Language, Literacy and Arts Education at the University of Melbourne.

Nicolas Brasch
Amanda Dawson

Contents

Chapter 1

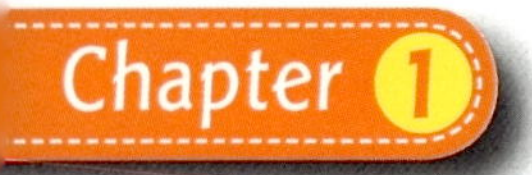

King of a Large Land

A long, long time ago
there lived a king.

His name was King Midas,
and he ruled over a large land.

He was a good king,
much loved by his people,
but he had one downfall.

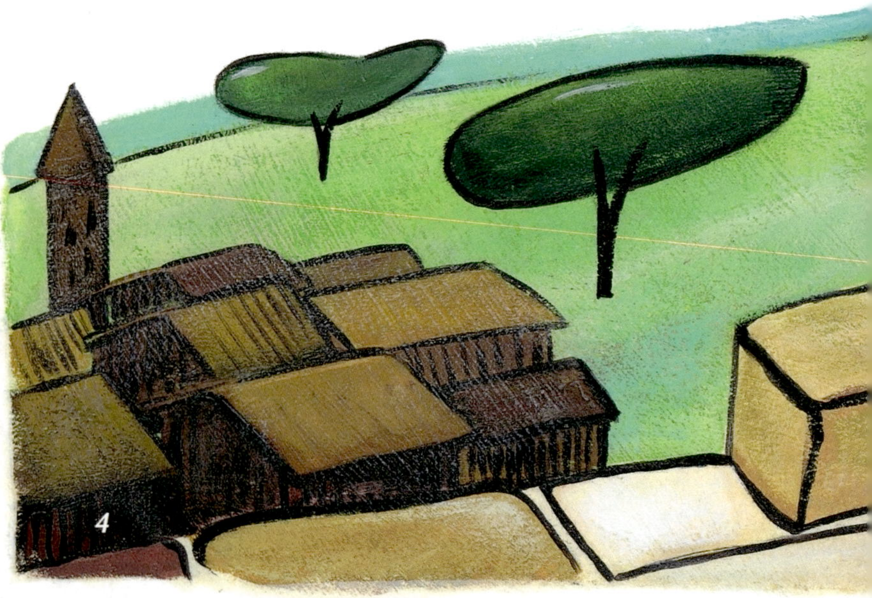

He knew that other kings had far more money than he did, and he wished that he was as rich as them.

One day, King Midas was walking through his palace garden when he saw a man asleep in a flower bed.

King Midas woke the man and asked, "What are you doing here?"

The man got a shock.

He had never met the king before
and he knew that he was in big trouble.

"I have no money for food or shelter,"
the man told the king.
"I have nowhere else to go."

Chapter 2

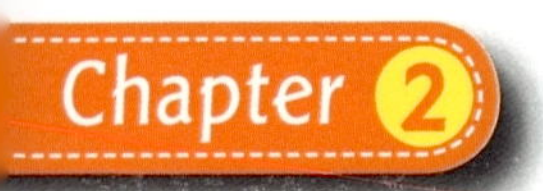

An Act of Kindness

King Midas took pity on the man and took him back to the palace.

There, he made sure that the man had lots of food and drink.
He also gave him a warm bed to sleep in, for ten days.

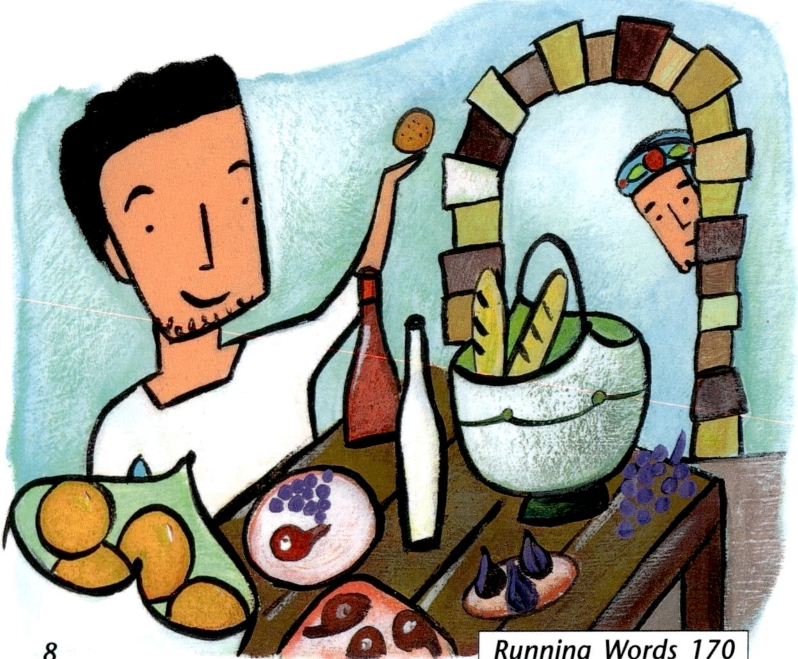

Running Words 170

At the end of the ten days,
King Midas gave the man some money
and sent him on his way.

The man was very grateful.

Watching over this act of kindness
was Dionysus, one of the Gods.

Dionysus appeared before King Midas
and said, "Your act of kindness
will be rewarded.
I grant you one wish."

King Midas saw that, finally, he had a chance to be richer than all the other kings he knew.

"I want everything I touch to turn to gold," he told Dionysus.

"I'm not sure that's such a good idea," Dionysus said.
"Are you sure you don't want something else?"

"No, that's what I want," King Midas said.

So Dionysus granted King Midas his wish.

Chapter 3

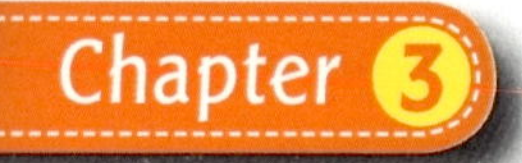

The Golden Touch

King Midas decided to try out
his new power.
He reached down and picked up a rock.
It turned to gold.

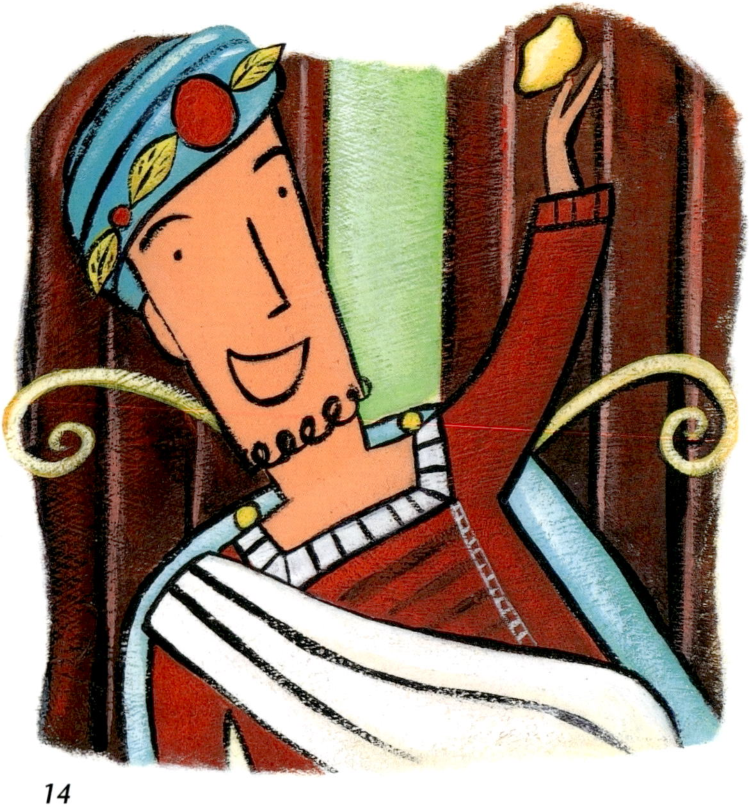

He picked a flower,
and it turned to gold, too.

"This is fantastic!"
King Midas said to himself.

At dinner time, King Midas sat
in front of a huge feast.
His excitement had made him
very hungry.
But as he picked up a chicken leg,
it turned to gold.
He could not eat it.

Then he grabbed a bunch of grapes
and it turned to gold, too.

King Midas called for his daughter.
When she arrived, he said,
"Please feed me or I will starve."

The king's daughter picked up a fig and put it in the king's mouth. As he ate the fig, he touched his daughter's hand. She turned to gold.

"Oh no!" he screamed. "What have I done?"

Chapter 4

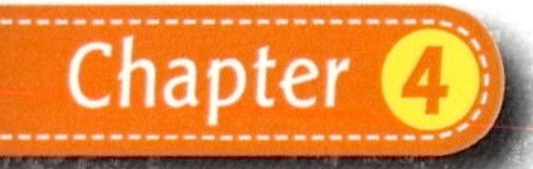

Happily Ever After

King Midas called out to Dionysus.
Dionysus appeared before him again.

"Please remove my wish!"
pleaded the King.
"I was so greedy and now I am
so unhappy."

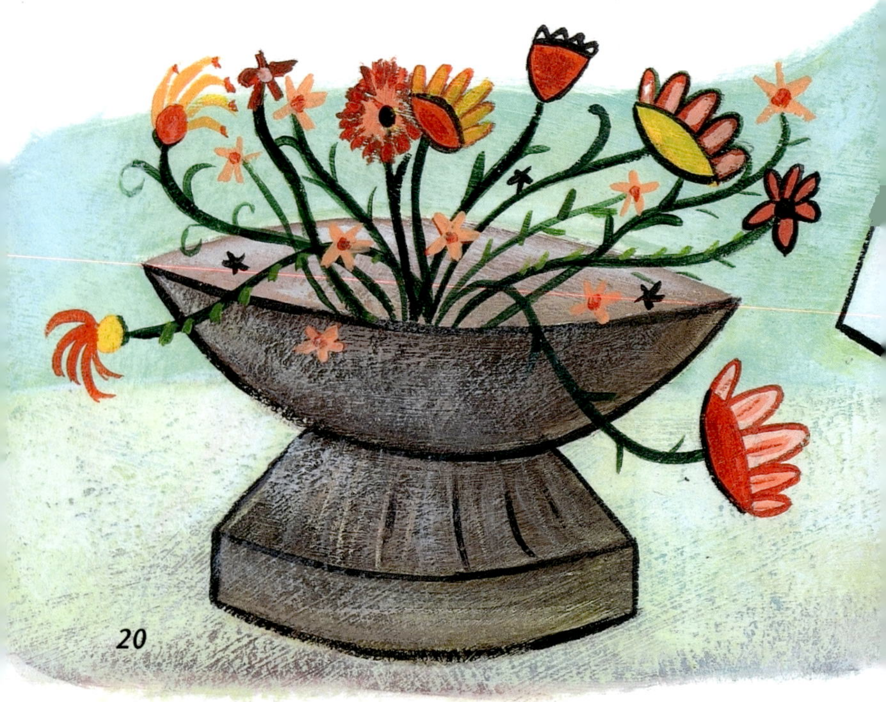

"I can remove your wish," Dionysus told him. "But if I do, you will be poorer than you were before."

"That's fine," said King Midas. "Please do it now."

Dionysus removed the wish.

King Midas was poorer than
he had ever been before,
but he was much happier as well.

Unlike many kings,
he now knew that there were far more
important things than money.